Girl TALK

Book of COOKING

Anyone can go and buy food in packets and tins, but not everyone can cook up delicious dishes that are lots of fun to do and a pleasure to eat. Turn the page to find tons of yummy dishes for you to create for your family and friends…

First published in 1998 by BBC Worldwide Ltd
Woodlands, 80 Wood Lane, London W12 0TT

Girl Talk copyright © BBC Magazines 1995
All rights reserved

Text by Moira Butterfield
copyright © BBC Worldwide Ltd 1998
Illustrations by Louise Comfort
and Maggie Sayer
copyright © BBC Worldwide Ltd 1998
Design by Full Steam Ahead
ISBN 0 563 38097 7
Printed by Cambus Litho, East Kilbride

BBC

Be A Cooking Superstar!

Don't like spices?
If you don't like the taste of spices such as garlic or chilli, just leave them out. YOU DECIDE how you want your food to taste!

The recipes in this book have been carefully chosen and tested out to guarantee you results that everyone will want to eat again and again. Good luck and good eating!

Don't like nuts?
Some people find that nuts make them ill, so check first before you serve any recipe that contains them.

Contents

SYMBOLS TO HELP YOU

You'll see these pictures by the recipes. They'll help you choose what you want to make:

❖ Cooking needed

❖ No cooking needed

❖ Chopping needed (Ask an adult to help you or do this for you)

❖ Serve cold

❖ Serve hot

START HERE

Read this section first to make sure you get the best from your Girl Talk Book of Cooking. It contains some important tips that will help you on your mission to become a brilliant cook.

COOK'S CRUCIAL BOOK OF RULES

❖ Wash your hands before you start.

❖ Wear an apron to protect your clothes.

❖ Check with the adults you look after to see if it's OK to cook. Read

KEEP ON COOKING

Like most hobbies, the best way to learn cooking is to practise. Ask if you can prepare one dish a week, perhaps at the weekend when there's plenty of time. That way you'll get to try out all the recipes in the book.

WEIGHING AND MEASURING

It's important to get the right amount of ingredients for each recipe. The measurements in this book are written in metric and imperial. **WARNING**: Choose your method of measuring and then stick to it – **NEVER** mix the two.

Metric
g = gram
ml = millilitre
(for measuring liquids)

Imperial
oz = ounce
lb = pound
fl oz = fluid ounce
(for measuring liquids)

Remember that when a recipe says 'one teaspoon' or 'one tablespoon' it means one level spoonful, not one heaped-up with ingredients.

ALL ABOUT OVENS

Electric ovens measure heat in Fahrenheit (°F), or Centigrade (°C).
Gas ovens measure heat in Marks (for instance, Mark 3). All three heat measurements are in this book. Choose the one that's right for your oven.

through the recipe with them to check that you've got all the things you need. Then keep an adult handy to help with any difficult bits.

❖ Make sure that you don't leave a mess when you've finished. If you do, your cooking days could be over pretty quickly!

❖ Put on oven gloves if you ever handle a warm dish or tin. Otherwise you could easily burn your hands.

TOP CHEF TIPS

As you cook your way through the delicious recipes in this book, you'll also come across some helpful tips and advice. Here are two essential basics to learn before you start.

How to grease a baking tin

1 Rub some greaseproof paper on a pat of butter or margarine.

2 Then spread the paper all around the tin. This will stop food sticking to the tin when it's cooking.

How to separate an egg

1 Knock an egg gently on the side of a bowl to crack the shell slightly.

2 Hold the egg over the bowl and pull the shell apart along the crack.

3 Pass the yolk back and forth between the two shell halves, letting the egg white drop into the bowl. When all the white has drained off, place the yolk in a separate bowl.

Super Snacks And Dips

Yummy potato skins

Serve these crunchy potato pieces on a plate with some dips to dunk them into.

Ingredients
- 5 baked potatoes
- Olive oil
- Salt

1 When you have baked the potatoes, leave the oven on at the same setting.

2 Let the potatoes cool slightly, then ask an adult to cut them into quarters. Use a teaspoon to scoop out some of the inside flesh, leaving a thin layer of the potato on the skins. Save the inside flesh to make potato cakes the next day.

3 Lay the potato skins in a shallow baking dish or tray. Gently drizzle a little olive oil over them (or brush it on with a pastry brush) and sprinkle them with salt.

4 Return them to the oven for 20 minutes until they go brown and crisp.

Make yourself a popular person by offering to rustle up some tasty snacks for your family.

Pick a Potato

Baked potatoes are healthy, cheap and easy to do! Scrub the potato and prick its skin all over with a fork. Bake in the oven at 200°C (400°F, Mark 6) for 1–1¼ hrs. When it's ready it will feel soft if you squeeze it. The bigger the potato, the longer it will take to cook.

Fantastic fillings

Cheesy potato: Cut the potato in half. Scoop out the insides and mash them up with a knob of butter, a splash of milk and some grated cheese. Pile the mixture back in the potato skins, grate some more cheese on top and grill until the top browns.

Bacon cheesy potato: Make a cheesy potato but put a slice of streaky bacon over the top of each half instead of grated cheese. Grill until the bacon is crispy.

Spicy bean potato: Mix baked beans with a teaspoon of Worcestershire sauce. Heat them up and pour them over the potato halves.

Summer topping: Mix some cottage cheese with chopped-up fruit such as pineapple chunks. If you like, add a handful of peanuts, too. Pile the mixture on top of the potato halves.

Dollop on any of the cold dip ideas from page 7.

Potato cakes

Serve these tasty golden potato patties as snacks with a main meal. This recipe makes about

Ingredients
- Mashed-up potato from the 5 baked potatoes used to make potato skins, or mash from 5 boiled potatoes.
- 110 g (4 oz) grated Cheddar cheese (ask an adult to help)
- 1 chopped-up spring onion or some chives
- 2 eggs

1 Turn on the oven to 190°C (375°F, Mark 5).

BREAD SNACKS

PERFECT CHEESE ON TOAST

Lots of people cook cheese on toast, but this special recipe is a cut above the rest. The pinches of mustard powder and Worcestershire sauce add a delicious tangy flavour to the toast topping.

Ingredients for two slices
- 110 g (4 oz) grated Cheddar cheese (ask an adult to help)
- 2 tablespoons milk
- A pinch of salt and pepper
- ½ teaspoon Worcestershire sauce
- ½ teaspoon mustard powder
- 2 slices of bread

1 Mix the cheese to a paste with the milk, salt and pepper, Worcestershire sauce and mustard.

2 Put the bread under the grill and toast it lightly on one side.

3 Spread the mixture on the toasted side and grill it until it is golden and bubbling.

4 If you like, use tomato slices to make a face on top of the mixture before you grill it.

2 Mix the mashed potato, cheese, and spring onion with 1 egg.

3 Scoop out handfuls of potato mixture and shape them into little rounded cakes about 7 cm (3 in) across.

4 Put the cakes on a greased baking sheet and use a pastry brush to coat first one side, then the other with beaten egg.

5 Bake in the oven for 20 minutes, until golden brown.

HOT TUNA SLICES

Ingredients for 2 slices
- 75 g (3 oz) tinned tuna
- 1 teaspoon of your favourite pickle
- 1 teaspoon of mayonnaise
- Butter or margarine spread
- 2 slices of bread
- 2 slices Cheddar cheese

1 Mix the tuna, pickle and mayonnaise.

2 Butter the bread and spread the tuna mixture over it. Lay a slice of cheese on top.

3 Grill until the cheese melts.

DO THE DIPS

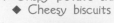

Mix a large pot of cottage cheese or a 225 g (8 oz) tub of cream cheese with a dessertspoon of mayonnaise and 225 g (8 oz) of crème fraîche. Add a pinch of salt and some pepper. Then experiment with adding flavours to find your favourite dips. Here are some ideas to try.

- ◆ Chopped chives and herbs
- ◆ Flaked tuna and a small, drained tin of sweetcorn
- ◆ Chopped clove of garlic
- ◆ Tomato paste or a small can of drained, chopped tomatoes
- ◆ Crumbled or grated cheese
- ◆ Mustard
- ◆ Dessertspoon of chutney
- ◆ Curry powder
- ◆ Chopped-up cucumber

Serve dips in pretty pots on plates covered with paper napkins. Around the pots lay finger food for dipping:

- ◆ Pitta bread sliced into fingers
- ◆ Crisps
- ◆ Crispy potato skins
- ◆ Cheesy biscuits

TOP
SANDWICH FILLINGS

- Cream cheese mixed with chopped ham, chives, crunchy vegetable pieces or chopped-up pineapple.

- Mashed-up tuna with herbs sprinkled on. Add some sweetcorn for more crunch.

- Cooked chicken mixed with mayonnaise, a pinch of curry powder and a sprinkling of sultanas. Try mixing in a dessertspoon of peanut butter, too.

- Slice of ham, slice of cheese, slice of tomato. Keep going until your sandwich is as big as you want!

- Cheese and apple slices sprinkled with lemon juice to stop them going brown.

- Hard-boiled egg with salad. Add crunchy bacon bits, too.

- Cottage cheese mixed with a sliced-up peach or pear.

- Grated cheese mixed into a paste with a small chopped-up tomato.

- Your own sandwich filling recipe. Write it here.

....

....

The Ultimate Packed Lunch

If you take a packed lunch to school, try some of these ideas to make your eating more exciting!

SUPER SALAD BOX

Get a small plastic storage box that you can fit in your lunchbox. Fill it with different salads to make your lunch extra-interesting and healthy.

- Next time you have cooked rice, ask to keep some back to make a cold rice salad. Mix it with chopped-up fruit such as a slice of orange or apple, diced ham or hard-boiled egg. Add a teaspoon of mayonnaise or a teaspoon of honey mixed with a little vinegar.

- Chop up a carrot and crunch on the little pieces.

- Cut up some cold boiled potato and mix it with mayonnaise and chopped-up chives.

- Shred lettuce so that it fits in the box and mix it with a chopped-up slice of orange.

Lunchbox Italian-style

Cold cooked pasta shapes such as shells make a tasty energy-packed salad that you can take to school instead of sandwiches. Try these variations with your favourite pasta shapes:

- Pasta plus ribbons of sliced cooked ham, cold cooked peas or sweetcorn and mayonnaise mixed with an equal amount of plain yoghurt.

- Pasta plus flaked tuna and some Thousand Island dressing – 2 teaspoons of mayonnaise mixed with 1 teaspoon of tomato ketchup, 1 teaspoon of yoghurt and a dash of lemon juice.

A Boxful of Health

When you eat you give your body the building materials that it uses to help it grow and stay healthy. If you give your body bad building materials, it won't be able to do the job! Give your body the right things every day by putting these in your lunchbox...

- [ ] Fresh fruit or vegetables (such as salad).

- [ ] Protein (from cheese, meat, nuts, fish or eggs).

- [ ] Fibre (from food with grains in it, such as granary bread or muesli bars).

- [ ] Water. Choose a drink made at home with water instead of a fizzy can or carton.

PUDDING PLEASE

Buy a plain yoghurt (Greek yoghurt is ideal) or a fromage frais and mix in one or more of the magic ingredients shown below. Put it into a secure plastic box that fits into your lunchbox.

Mini marshmallows

Chopped-up fruit and a dessertspoon of desiccated coconut

Chocolate raisins

Crunched-up chocolate cookie pieces (put them in just before you eat the yoghurt).

Teaspoon of honey

HEALTHY FRIDGE MAGNETS

Make these fridge magnets to remind everyone to eat healthily. It'll also remind you to think of good food to pack in your lunchbox.

WHAT YOU'LL NEED
- Stiff plain card
- Mini magnets (buy these from craft shops)
- Pencil and scissors
- Paint and paintbrush
- PVA glue

1 Draw shapes on the card, such as a strawberry, a carrot or a fish. Cut them out.

3 When the paint is dry, coat the card with PVA glue. When it dries it will give a shiny protective coating.

4 Glue a mini magnet to the back of each piece of card.

2 Write a healthy food message on each one and paint it brightly.

BEAN SALAD

Make a bowl of this the day before you want to eat it, because the flavour is better the next day. Store it in a cool place until you're ready to tuck in.

Ingredients

* 1 400 g (14 oz) tin of flageolet beans
* 1 400 g (14 oz) tin of red kidney beans
* 225 ml (8 fl oz) vinegar
* 110 g (4 oz) white sugar
* 110 ml (4 fl oz) olive oil
* Salt and pepper
* 2 medium-sized mild onions

1. Ask an adult to open the cans of beans and drain them. Ask them to cut up the onions into rings.

2. Pour the flageolet and kidney beans into a colander and run water over them to wash them.

3. Mix the vinegar, sugar, oil, salt and pepper. Pour the mixture over the beans and stir in the onions.

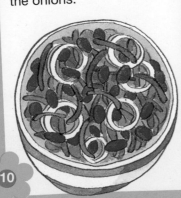

Sunny Summer Days

When the weather is warm, make some outdoor food to eat with barbecues and picnics. Impress everyone by offering to make a fantastic salad or a pudding!

Sunshine salad

Make this unusual but delicious salad a few hours before eating it, so that the marshmallows dissolve.

Ingredients

* 225 ml (8 fl oz) soured cream or crème fraîche
* 175 g (6 oz) tiny marshmallows
* 3 tablespoons shredded coconut
* 1 200g (7 oz) tin of pineapple chunks
* 1 200g (7 oz) tin of mandarin oranges

1. Mix the cream or crème fraîche, marshmallows and coconut. Leave the mixture in the fridge for a couple of hours.

2. Ask an adult to open and drain the cans of fruit. Stir them into the mixture.

The recipe game

Try this fun cooking game with a friend and taste each other's creations! Choose 4 items from the following list. Then make up a recipe using your 4 items. Write it down, collect the ingredients and then try it out!

* Banana * Raisins * Plain yoghurt
* Apple * Orange * Piece of cheese

* Roll or bread slice * Butter or margarine * Tomato

* Tomato sauce * Mayonnaise * Pot of jam * Honey

* Small sponge fingers * Packet of cornflakes * Tin of golden syrup

* Tin of drinking chocolate * Carton of milk

If you invent any good recipes, stick them in the special section on pages 46-47!

Incredibly Easy Mousse

This mousse is great for summer meals and it really works brilliantly!

Ingredients
* Box of fruit-flavoured jelly squares
* 1 225g (8 oz) tub of cream cheese

Simply make up 275 ml (½ pint) of fruit-flavoured jelly and when it is just about to set mix in the cream cheese. Chill it and then eat it! Yes, it's **that** easy! (Leaving you with more time for fun in the sun.)

SIDESALAD SECRETS

Decorate a salad bowl with these 2 ideas:

■ To make flower-shaped slices of cucumber, drag a fork down the outside skin before the cucumber gets sliced.

■ Trim up spring onions and cut around the tops with scissors. Lay them in a bowl of water filled with ice cubes and leave them until the tops have curled out like little palm trees.

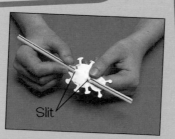

LOVELY LEMON SQUASH

Serve this refreshing drink in a glass with minty ice cubes and a straw bug.

Ingredients for 1 glass

 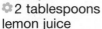

* 2 tablespoons lemon juice
* 2 teaspoons sugar
* 150 ml (¼ pint) can of soda water

1 Put the lemon juice and sugar into a glass.

2 Fill it to the top with soda water. Stir the drink well and taste it. Put more lemon juice in if you want it to taste stronger.

Straw bug

Make a funny straw bug to decorate your drinking glass.

Slit

WHAT YOU'LL NEED
* Some plain card
* Pencil and scissors
* Felt-tips or crayons

1 Copy this straw bug shape onto card. Cut round the outline and make 2 slits as shown.

2 Decorate your bug and slip it onto a plastic straw.

Slit

Food To Warm You Up!

When it's chilly outside, warm to these hot food ideas.

SIZZLING SAUCES

Serve tasty barbecue-flavour gravy with a meaty meal instead of ordinary gravy. Serve the hot honey sauce with beefburgers, pork chops or on cooked rice.

Barbecue Gravy

Makes 150 ml (¼ pint)

Ingredients
* 1 teaspoon tomato paste
* 2 tablespoons red wine vinegar
* 2 tablespoons brown sugar
* 2 tablespoons Worcestershire sauce
* 150 ml (¼ pint) water

1. Stir all the ingredients in a saucepan over a low heat until everything has blended together.

2. Bring to the boil and let the gravy bubble gently for 10 minutes.

HOT HONEY SAUCE

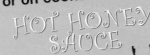

"Honey sauce is yummy on burgers and bangers!"

Makes 150 ml (¼ pint)

Ingredients
* 110 ml (4 fl oz) water
* 2 teaspoons cornflour
* 2 teaspoons lemon juice
* 2 teaspoons soy sauce
* 4 teaspoons tomato ketchup
* 2 tablespoons honey

1. Mix all the ingredients in a cup, except for the honey.

2. Put the honey in a saucepan and heat it gently until it starts to bubble. Mix in the other ingredients and let the mixture bubble for a minute.

MARINADE HEAVEN

A marinade is a tasty liquid that you normally soak meat in overnight in the fridge. These marinades could also be used for soaking vegetables, then making delicious kebabs with cubes of courgettes, peppers, parsnips or onions. Cut the vegetables to about the same size and boil them for a minute or two before marinating. Leave the kebabs in the marinade for about 30 minutes and then grill for about 10 minutes. The taste of the marinade comes out when the meat or vegetables are cooked.

LEMON HERB MARINADE

Ingredients
* 110 ml (4 fl oz) olive oil
* 55 ml (2 fl oz) lemon juice
* 55 ml (2 fl oz) white wine vinegar
* 2 teaspoons fresh chopped parsley (ask an adult to do the chopping)
* 2 teaspoons fresh chives snipped with scissors into little pieces
* Grated rind of a lemon (ask an adult to help you)
* 1 tablespoon of chopped fresh rosemary or 1 teaspoon dried rosemary

1. Mix everything in a bowl and pour it over some meat in a shallow glass dish. Make sure all the meat is covered.

TERIYAKE MARINADE

Ingredients
* 110 ml (4 fl oz) soy sauce
* 75 g (3 oz) clear honey
* 1 clove of crushed garlic (ask an adult to do this) or a teaspoon of ready-prepared garlic
* ½ teaspoon of ground ginger

2. Leave the meat to marinate for a few hours (preferably overnight) before the meat gets cooked.

VICTORIA'S MINI SPONGES

These little sponges are lovely eaten hot with custard or ice cream.

Ingredients for 6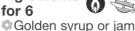

* Golden syrup or jam
* Glacé cherries
* 150 g (5 oz) margarine
* 150 g (5 oz) caster sugar
* 3 beaten eggs
* 150 g (5 oz) self-raising flour
* Pinch of salt
* Milk

1 Put the oven on at 180°C (350°F, Mark 4). Lightly grease six little ramekin dishes and put them on a baking tray.

A ramekin dish

2 Add a tablespoon of syrup or jam to each one. Cut cherries in half and put one half upside-down in the middle of each dish.

3 Beat together the margarine and the sugar until smooth.

4 Mix in the eggs and salt, then add the flour a little at a time. Add a tablespoon of milk if you need to, to make it soft and smooth so it drops off the spoon.

5 Spoon 3 or 4 tablespoons into the dishes (not to the top, as they will rise a little when cooked).

6 Cook for 15-20 minutes until risen and golden.

7 Ask an adult to slide a knife round the edge of each dish and put a plate on top, then turn the ramekin dish upside-down to get the sponge out. Be careful, the syrup or jam will be very hot at first.

Chilli for Chilly Days

Serve chilli with plain rice. Ask an adult to put the chilli powder in or, if you prefer, leave it out altogether.

Ingredients

* 450 g (1 lb) beef, lamb or vegetarian quorn mince
* 1 onion (ask an adult to chop it up)
* 50 g (2 oz) tomato paste
* 1 big can of baked beans
* 1 teaspoon chilli powder
* 2 tablespoons milk
* Pepper and salt
* 1 dessertspoon brown sugar

1 Ask an adult to help you brown the mince in a frying pan. Stir it round with a wooden spatula until it is brown all over.

2 Put the mince in a big saucepan and add the other ingredients. Stir them round and let them cook gently until the meat is tender (about an hour).

FOOD FOR THE BIRDS

Birds have a hard time finding food in winter. You can help them by leaving out crumbs and scraps such as chopped bacon rind, or hanging a bird-feeder up where they can reach it (make sure it's too high for any neighbourhood cats to get at).

1 Make a feeder from a net bag used for selling vegetables in supermarkets.

2 Fill it with unsalted peanuts.

3 Tie round the top with string and hang it up.

WINTER WARMER

Next time you have a hot drink such as hot chocolate, stir it with a fragrant-smelling cinnamon stick.

ALL ABOUT PROTEIN

You need to eat PROTEIN so your body can grow and repair itself. But where do you find it? Try and think of some protein-rich foods, then check the list below to see if you're on the right lines!

* Fish
* Lean meat
* Cheese
* Eggs
* Nuts and beans
* Soya
* Milk

BREADS AROUND THE WORLD

There are lots of different types of bread. Here's a list to check against next time you go to the supermarket.

◆ **French baguette** – Long, stick of white bread. It doesn't stay fresh for long, so eat it on the day you buy it.

◆ **Irish soda bread** – A spongy bread made from wheat flour and buttermilk.

◆ **Pitta bread** – Greek bread that's great for filling, and packing, in lunchboxes.

◆ **Foccacia** – A moist Italian flat bread usually eaten warm with all kinds of toppings. Try it with cheese and grilled bacon on top.

◆ **Wholemeal bread** – Brown bread made with healthy wholemeal flour.

◆ **Naan bread** – Delicious Indian bread. Eat it warm, brushed with melted butter.

◆ **German rye bread** – A dark strong-flavoured bread made from pure rye flour.

My favourite bread

....

Brilliant Bread

Bread is eaten all over the world. Join in with these tasty ideas.

TOMATO CHEESE ROLLS

This recipe makes about 20 mini rolls that are delicious with butter.

Ingredients
✿ 225 g (8 oz) plain flour
✿ 1 tablespoon baking powder
✿ 50 g (2 oz) butter or margarine
✿ 1 teaspoon salt
✿ 225 g (8 oz) grated cheese (ask an adult to help)
✿ 1 200 g (7 oz) tin of chopped, drained tomatoes
✿ Milk to brush the rolls

1. Grease a baking sheet and put the oven on at 230°C (450°F, Mark 8). Sprinkle some flour onto a board, ready for your bread.

2. Put the flour, baking powder, butter and salt in a bowl. Make sure your hands are clean first, then rub the mixture lightly together with your fingers until it looks like breadcrumbs.

3. Add the cheese and the tomatoes. Stir the mixture until it makes one ball of dough.

4. Turn the dough onto the floured board and knead it for 2 minutes.

5. Pull off golf-ball-sized pieces of the dough and shape them into sausages. Put them on the tray and use a pastry brush to coat them with milk (this will help them go a golden-brown colour). Bake for 15 minutes and eat hot or cold.

BANANA NUT BREAD

This bread is really a kind of cake that you can slice up and butter. If you prefer, leave out the nuts.

Ingredients
- 75 g (3 oz) butter or margarine
- 175 g (6 oz) caster sugar
- 2 eggs
- 275 g (10 oz) bananas (weigh them with the skins removed)
- 225 g (8 oz) plain flour – sieved with the baking powder and salt
- 3 level teaspoons baking powder
- ½ teaspoon salt
- 50 g (2 oz) chopped nuts

1. Put the oven on at 180°C (350°F, Mark 4). Grease a standard-sized loaf tin.

2. Beat the butter and sugar together until soft. Do this in a bowl with a wooden spoon, or in a food processor. Then slowly beat the eggs in.

3. Mash the bananas and mix them in. Then add the flour and the nuts. Stir everything together and pour the mixture into the loaf tin.

4. Bake for an hour or until the top has browned well. When the loaf has cooled, turn it out onto a board and ask an adult to slice it. Butter the slices and serve on a plate.

BREAD AND BUTTER PUDDING

This is a delicious way to use up stale bread slices.

Ingredients
- 4 slices of bread
- 25 g (1 oz) butter
- 1 tablespoon brown sugar
- 50 g (2 oz) sultanas, raisins or currants
- 425 ml (¾ pint) milk
- 2 eggs
- ¼ teaspoon cinnamon

1. Put the oven on at 180°C (350°F, Mark 4).

2. Butter one side of the bread slices and lay 2 of them, butter side up, in a 850 ml (1½ pint) ovenproof dish. Sprinkle on half the sugar and fruit. Then lay the other 2 bread slices on top and sprinkle on the rest of the sugar and fruit.

3. Whisk together the milk and the eggs. If you like spices, add a pinch of cinnamon. Pour the custard mixture over the bread and bake the pudding for 45 minutes, until the custard sets.

Cream Cheese Bread

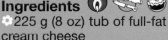

Here's a brilliant way to serve pieces of French bread. If you like garlic, use garlic-flavoured cream cheese.

Ingredients
- 225 g (8 oz) tub of full-fat cream cheese
- Bunch of fresh herbs – choose from parsley, thyme, mint, basil, marjoram or dill. Mix them up if you like, then ask an adult to chop them. Alternatively use 2 teaspoons of dried herbs instead.
- Salt and pepper
- 1 French baguette

1. Put the oven on at 200°C (400°F, Mark 6).

2. Put the cheese into a bowl and beat it with a wooden spoon to make it soft. Mix in the herbs, salt and pepper.

3. Ask an adult to slice all along the French loaf. They shouldn't slice right through.

4. Spread the cream cheese mixture between each slice. Then wrap the loaf in foil. If it is too big to fit in your oven, you may have to do it in 2 halves.

5. Cook the loaf for 25 minutes. Ask an adult to unwrap the loaf and separate the slices.

ALL ABOUT CARBOHYDRATES

Carbohydrates give your body energy, so they're really important. Look for recipes on these pages containing bread, potatoes, rice and pasta – starchy carbohydrates that will give you bags of get up and go!

EASY VEGETABLE RICE

Ingredients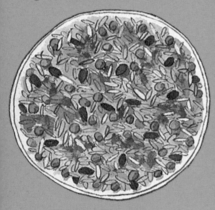

* 225 g (8 oz) hot cooked rice (ask an adult to do this and keep it warm by leaving the lid on the saucepan)
* 1 200 g (7 oz) tin of sweetcorn
* 1 200 g (7 oz) tin of chopped, drained tomatoes
* Handful of sultanas
* 110 g (4 oz) cooked peas
* 110 g (4 oz) grated cheese (ask an adult to help), or 150 ml (¼ pint) of hot honey sauce

Mix all the ingredients into the rice before you serve it up. If you like, stir in the honey sauce from page 12 instead of the grated cheese.

CARROT PURÉE

Next time you have boiled carrots on the menu put the cooked carrots in a food processor and whiz them round to make a paste called a purée. Mix the purée with a dash of cream, milk or crème fraîche and add salt and pepper.

Get Wise, Eat Veg!

Vegetables help you to stay healthy, so eat LOTS! Cook up some winners that will make eating them a pleasure.

BRILLIANT BASIC CHEESE SAUCE FOR VEGETABLES

Put cooked vegetables such as cauliflower in an ovenproof dish and pour this sauce over them. Then brown the dish under the grill. Use this sauce on pasta, too.

Ingredients

* 50 g (2 oz) butter or margarine
* 50 g (2 oz) white or wholemeal flour
* 570 ml (1 pint) milk
* Salt and pepper
* 110 g (4 oz) grated cheese (ask an adult to help)

1 Melt the butter in a saucepan. Then take the saucepan off the heat.

2 Use a wooden spoon to stir in the flour. It will make a paste called a *roux*. Put it back on the heat and cook it for about 2 minutes, stirring all the time.

3 Gradually pour in the milk, stirring constantly. When you've whisked it smooth, slowly bring the sauce to the boil, stirring all the time. It will gradually thicken. Now add the salt and pepper.

4 When the sauce is thick, add the cheese. It will melt into the sauce.

VEGETABLE PASTIES

These are perfect eaten cold in a packed lunch or hot for dinner with savoury gravy.

Ingredients
for 5 pasties
* 450 g (1 lb) freezer packet of stewing vegetables (this usually includes carrots, turnips, potatoes and mini onions), cooked as per instructions (usually boiled in a saucepan)
* 110 g (4 oz) grated cheese (ask an adult to help)
* 1 teaspoon dried sage, or 1 teaspoon mango chutney (if you like a slightly curried taste)
* Salt and pepper
* 450 g (1 lb) packet shortcrust pastry

1. Put the oven on to 200°C (400°F, Mark 6). Sprinkle some flour on a board and rub some flour onto a rolling pin.

2. Mix the vegetables, cheese and sage or chutney with a sprinkling of salt and pepper.

3. Roll the pastry out on the board. When you think it is thin enough, use a teacup saucer as a cutter guide and cut out as many circles as you can. You will need to reroll the pastry a couple of times. Brush round the edges of the circles with water.

4. Spoon some filling into the centre of each round and bring the edges up together to make a pasty. Pinch round the top edge with your finger and thumb to seal it. Use a pastry brush to coat the pasties with a little milk.

5. Put the pasties on a baking sheet and cook them for 15 minutes. Then turn the oven down to 170°C (325°F, Mark 3) and cook for a further 15 minutes, or until the pastry looks golden brown.

SCRUMPTIOUS CARROT SOUP

You need a food processor to make this delicious smooth soup.

Ingredients
* 50 g (2 oz) butter
* 1 medium onion (finely chopped by an adult)
* 450 g (1 lb) carrots, peeled and chopped
* 570 ml (1 pint) vegetable stock (made with a cube and hot water)
* ½ teaspoon mixed herbs
* ½ bay-leaf
* Pinch of salt and pepper
* 570 ml (1 pint) milk

1. Put the butter in a large saucepan and melt it over a medium heat.

2. Add the chopped onion and carrots and cook for 10 minutes with the lid on the pan, stirring occasionally. Add the vegetable stock.

3. Stir in the herbs, bay-leaf, salt and pepper.

4. Put the lid back on and cook for another 10 minutes, stirring occasionally.

5. Take out the bay-leaf and ask an adult to liquidize the soup in the food processor to make it smooth. Then put it back in the pan and add the milk. Heat up the soup and serve.

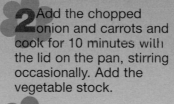

MEDITERRANEAN ROAST VEGETABLES

You've probably eaten roast potatoes and parsnips. Now try roasting some of the vegetables that people love to eat in the hot countries of Europe. They're delicious eaten hot or cold.

Ingredients
A selection from this list:
* Courgettes, washed and sliced in half lengthways, red or yellow bell peppers, cut in half with the seeds taken out, onions cut into quarters
* Olive oil
* Salt and pepper
* 1 clove of crushed garlic (ask an adult to do this)

1. Set the oven at 190°C (375°F, Mark 5)

2. Lay the vegetables on a big baking tray. Drizzle olive oil all over them and sprinkle on a little salt and pepper. If you like garlic, sprinkle on a crushed clove.

3. Bake the vegetables for about 45 minutes, until they are soft.

Special Tip: Try roasting sweet potato slices. Ask an adult to peel the sweet potatoes, boil them for 10 minutes and then slice them into rounds before you put them on the baking tray.

VEGETABLES ARE BRILLIANT!
Vegetables help you to stay healthy because they are full of vitamins and minerals, which your body needs. You'll get them if you eat a good balanced diet. That means lots of different healthy food, especially...vegetables!

TROPICAL FUN FRUIT SALAD

Make an exotic fruit salad using fruits that grow in hot places. Choose from passion fruit, bananas, pineapples, oranges, guavas and mangoes. Pick out an exciting selection from your local supermarket.

Ingredients
- Selection of fruit
- 150 ml (¼ pint) orange juice

1. First skin and chop up the fruit. You may need to ask an adult to do this part for you.

2. Stir all the fruit together in a bowl with the orange juice. Cover the bowl and refrigerate for at least half an hour before serving.

Fruity Fun!

Fruit is another health-giving food, so try to eat some every day. Here are some delicious fruit recipes to try on cooking days.

PEAR HEDGEHOGS

For a special pudding, serve pears covered in meringue and crunchy almonds. If you don't eat nuts, leave out the almonds.

Ingredients
- 1 400g (14 oz) tin of pear halves
- ½ teaspoon salt
- 2 egg whites (see page 5 for the best way to separate eggs)
- 110 g (4 oz) caster sugar
- 1 teaspoon cream of tartar
- 50 g (2 oz) flaked almonds (you can buy these in packets)
- A few raisins (optional)

1. Put the oven on at 140°C (275°F, Mark 1). Grease a baking tray.

2. Ask an adult to drain the pears and then place them flat side down on the tray.

3. Sprinkle the salt on the egg whites and whisk until they look stiff and make peaks in the bowl. Gradually sift in the sugar.

4. Mix the cream of tartar into the the meringue mixture and then use a knife to cover each pear with it.

5. Stick the almonds upright in the meringue mixture, all over the pears. Bake in the oven for 30 minutes, until the meringue is golden brown. Serve hot or cold. If you like, add raisins for eyes after cooking.

Barbecued Fruit

Next time you have a barbecue, surprise everyone with this delicious fruit treat. Alternatively, cook it under a hot grill.

Ingredients
✿ Selection of fruit such as pineapple rings, sliced peaches, pear halves, banana slices, sliced apples, apricot halves
✿ Brown sugar
✿ Butter
✿ Cinnamon (leave this out if you prefer)

1 Lay out a big square of foil that covers a grill pan. Put the fruit on it (don't pile fruit pieces on top of each other).

2 Sprinkle with the sugar and dot with small knobs of butter. Add the cinnamon too, if you like it.

3 Put another square of foil on top and roll up the edges of both pieces to seal in the fruit.

4 Grill for 15 minutes. Then ask an adult to unwrap the foil and spoon out the fruit. Serve hot.

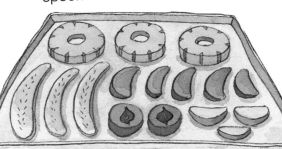

FRUITY PORK CHOPS

Pork goes well with the taste of fruit. Try it and see. Serve the pork with rice or mashed potatoes.

Ingredients for 4 people
🍴 2 big cooking apples
🍴 200 ml (⅓ pint) apple juice
🍴 50 g (2 oz) seedless raisins
🍴 1 tablespoon vegetable oil
🍴 4 pork chops

If you don't eat pork, grill some vegetarian sausages. Keep them separate while you make the sauce, then add the sausages to the pan 2 minutes from the end.

1 Ask an adult to peel, core and slice the cooking apples. Mix them with the apple juice and raisins.

2 Heat the oil in a large frying pan or a wok and fry the chops on both sides for about 5 minutes, until they look golden.

3 Add the apple mixture. Cover the pan and simmer gently for 30 minutes. Ask an adult to turn the chops once during that time.

4 Lift out the chops. Stir the apple mixture and spoon it on top of the meat.

FRUIT SEED JEWELLERY

1 Next time you eat a melon collect all the seeds from inside. Wash them and dry them on a tray in the airing cupboard, or outside if it's summer.

2 Thread a needle with some strong cotton and push it through the seeds to make a necklace or bracelet. Knot the thread securely together to keep the seeds on.

All about fibre

Fibre is a kind of carbohydrate that helps to keep your digestive system working well. That's the part of your body that uses up the food you eat, processing it and sending it off to the rest of your body. You find fibre in fruit, vegetables, wholemeal bread, wholegrain cereals, brown rice, beans and nuts.

19

Cook For The World

Every country in the world has its own traditional foods and favourite flavours. That's what makes cooking and eating so exciting! On the next six pages there are some wonderful recipes from around the world for you to try.

Hummus

SAVOURY DIP FROM GREECE

Give this delicious Greek dip to garlic-lovers. Serve it in a bowl with pitta bread fingers for dipping. You need a food processor or liquidizer to make Hummus.

Ingredients to make about 400 g (14 oz)
- 4 spring onions
- 1 clove of crushed garlic (ask an adult to do this)
- 1 400 g (14 oz) can of chick peas
- 225 g (8 oz) natural fromage frais
- 2 tablespoons lemon juice
- Salt and pepper

1 Use clean scissors to snip the spring onions into pieces.

2 Put all the ingredients into a food processor and blend them until smooth.

Couscous

SAVOURY SUPPER FROM ARAB LANDS

Couscous is a kind of grain. It's great for experimenting with because you can make it different every time you eat it by adding new ingredients.* Eat Couscous as a side dish instead of potatoes or vegetables, or make it a main meal by adding chopped cooked chicken to it just before you eat it.

Ingredients for 4 as a side dish. (Double the amounts to make a main meal for 4.)
- 570 ml (1 pint) vegetable stock (make this according to the stock cube packet instructions)
- 250 g (9 oz) couscous
- 2 tablespoons

cooking oil
- ½ large onion, finely chopped
- 1 clove of crushed garlic (ask an adult to prepare the garlix and the onion)
- 1 teaspoon ground cinnamon
- 1 400 g (14 oz) can of chick peas
- 1 tablespoon sultanas
- Other ingredients to choose from: handful of cashew nuts or almonds, sweetcorn, chopped red pepper, green peas

1 Make the stock and pour it over the couscous in a deep dish. Put the dish lid on or cover the dish with wrapping film and leave for at least

*You need to fry for this recipe. It's safest and easiest to do this in a large saucepan.

Huevos a la flamenca
TASTY EGGS AND TOMATOES FROM SPAIN

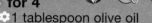

Use a lasagna tray for this delicious meal of eggs on tomato sauce. Serve the mixture with rice and make a Spanish side salad to go with it.

Ingredients for 4
- 1 tablespoon olive oil
- 1 chopped onion
- 2 400 g (14 oz) cans of chopped tomatoes
- 1 teaspoon dried oregano or basil (or buy tins of tomatoes with herbs already added to them)
- Salt and pepper
- Dash of Worcestershire sauce
- Pinch of chilli powder if you like a spicy taste
- 4 eggs

1 Put the oven on at 180°C (350°F, Mark 4).

2 Put the oil in a large saucepan and fry the onion gently for 2 minutes.

3 Add the tomatoes and cook for 10-15 minutes until the onion is soft.

4 Add the herbs, salt and pepper and Worcestershire sauce then cook for another 5 minutes. You can also add a touch of chilli powder if you like. Then pour the mixture into an ovenproof dish about 25 cm (10 in) across. Spread it out evenly.

5 Use the back of a spoon to make a shallow dip in the mixture. Break an egg into each hole. Then bake for about 20 minutes or until the eggs are set.

ENSALADE VERDE

Serve a bowlful of this simple Spanish salad with all sorts of dishes. Pour the dressing on just before you eat it.

Ingredients for one big bowl
- 1 crispy green lettuce
- 4 tomatoes, sliced across to make rings
- Bunch of spring onions (as many as you want), snipped up with scissors
- 3 tablespoons olive oil
- 1 tablespoon vinegar

(Spanish people usually use sherry or wine vinegar)

1 Wash the lettuce leaves and place them in the bowl.

2 Lay the tomatoes on top, then sprinkle the onion on.

3 Put the olive oil and vinegar in a screw-top jar. Screw the top on tightly and shake the jar until the dressing is mixed up. Pour over the salad or serve in a separate pouring dish.

10 minutes. The couscous will absorb the stock and then it will be ready to eat.

2 Put the oil in a big saucepan and fry the onion and garlic (if used).

3 Add all the other ingredients except for the couscous and cook gently for 10 minutes.

Add the couscous and stir in well. Cook gently for a couple of minutes serve warm.

10 AMAZING THINGS YOU NEVER KNEW ABOUT FOOD...

● Traditional Australian Aboriginal delicacies include wombat, lizard and witchetty grub, the giant juicy larva of an outback beetle.

● In some parts of Kenya after rain showers, the air gets filled with flying white ants. Local children gather the ants and take them home to fry for supper.

● Turkeys, potatoes and maize all originated in America. People in Europe did not discover them until the sixteenth and seventeenth centuries.

● Rice is the world's most popular food. Over 1,000 different varieties are grown in India alone.

21

10 AMAZING THINGS YOU NEVER KNEW ABOUT FOOD... continued

● The world's most popular drink is cola. Over 12 million cans are sold daily.

● Ice cream was invented by a French chef in the 1700s. Charles I, King of England at the time, loved it so much, he paid the chef a pension for the rest of his life.

At last!

● A doctor from St Louis in the USA invented peanut butter to make his patients feel happier and more healthy.

● The sandwich was actually invented by the Earl of Sandwich in the eighteenth century. His lordship felt peckish during a game of cards and devised the snack to keep him going until dinner!

● The Mongol people of the Russian Steppe region ate the first burgers in the 1200s. They munched on raw rissoles made of camel, goat or horse meat.

● The South American Aztecs introduced chocolate to the world. They enjoyed it in a rich cocoa drink.

PAIN PERDUE

TEATIME EGGY-BREAD FROM FRANCE

French children eat this delicious warm eggy-bread as a sweet or savoury snack. They add a sprinkling of sugar or some fruit, or a slice of ham, cheese or cooked bacon. You will need an adult to help you fry the pieces.

Ingredients for 3 slices of bread
✿ 3 thick slices of white bread, cut across the middle to make 6 triangles.
✿ 2 beaten eggs mixed with 150 ml (1/4 pint) milk
✿ Cooking oil

1 Soak the bread in the egg mixture for 5 minutes.

2 Heat a little oil and fry the pieces a batch at a time until golden brown on both sides.

ITALIAN PASTA SAUCE

FRESH TOMATO SAUCE FROM ITALY

Pasta is quick to cook and it's a healthy way to eat carbohydrates. Buy fresh pasta and cook it according to the instructions on the pack. Then drain it and mix it with this tasty fresh sauce. Use as much as you need and freeze the rest of the sauce for another meal.

Ingredients
✿ 2 tablespoons olive oil
✿ 1 crushed clove of garlic
✿ 2 large tins of chopped tomatoes
✿ 1 tablespoon chopped fresh herbs – such as oregano, basil and parsley.
✿ 1 teaspoon white sugar

Gently fry the crushed garlic in the oil for a few minutes, then add all the other ingredients and warm through.

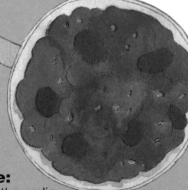

If you like:
◇ Leave out the garlic.
◇ Add a tablespoon of chopped onion.
◇ Stir in some sun-dried tomato paste for a richer flavour.
◇ Put some grated cheese on top of the pasta before you eat it.
◇ Make the sauce smooth in a food processor.

KOLACHES
MINI FRUITY PARCELS FROM
CENTRAL EUROPE

Sprinkle some icing sugar through a sieve onto these little parcels and serve them warm or cold anytime. Once you have made the pastry you need to leave it in the fridge for at least 3 hours to chill.

Ingredients
to make about 18
- 110 g (4 oz) cream cheese
- 110 g (4 oz) butter or margarine
- 225 g (8 oz) plain flour
- Pot of fruit jam or tin of fruit pie filling

1 Beat the cheese and butter together until the mixture is light and soft. Stir in the flour and leave the dough in the fridge for at least 3 hours.

2 When you're ready to make the kolaches put the oven on at 220°C (425°F, Mark 7). Grease a couple of flat baking sheets.

3 Sprinkle some flour onto a clean breadboard and sprinkle some onto a rolling pin. Roll out the dough quite thickly and cut it into 8 cm (3½ in) squares.

4 Put a teaspoonful of filling in the middle of each square. Dip a pastry brush in a teacup of water and wet round the edges of each square.

5 Fold the corners of the square up to the middle and pinch the edges together to seal them. Bake for 20 minutes, until the pastry looks golden.

FRUIT PAVLOVA
FRUIT MERINGUE FROM
AUSTRALIA & NEW ZEALAND

A pavlova is a big sticky meringue filled with fruit and cream. In this recipe you turn the oven OFF to cook the meringue overnight! When you make the base you will have 4 egg yolks left over. Mix them with a little milk and ask an adult to show you how to scramble them for tea.

Ingredients
- 4 egg whites
- 225 g (8 oz) caster sugar
- Whipping or double cream
- Fresh fruit such as strawberries, kiwifruit or seedless grapes

1 Turn the oven on to 200°C (400°F, Mark 6). Grease a baking sheet or lay a piece of baking parchment (non-stick cooking paper) on it.

2 Beat the egg whites until the mixture is stiff and makes peaks in the bowl.

3 Beat in the sugar a little at a time. Then spoon the mixture onto the baking sheet and shape it like a round nest.

4 Put the meringue quickly inside the oven and then turn it OFF. Leave overnight without opening the oven door (to keep the heat in). As the oven slowly cools, it will cook the meringue.

5 Put the meringue carefully on a dish and fill it with whipped double cream. Then pile the fruit on top.

Cook For The World

TACOS

CRUNCHY SHELLS WITH A SAVOURY FILLING FROM MEXICO

Buy a box of taco shells and make this mixture to go inside them (get an adult to help you with the frying). Make it as spicy or as mild as you like. If you don't eat beef, replace the mince with Quorn mince, which works just as well. When you serve the shells, put dishes of extra ingredients on the dinner table for people to finish 'building' their own tacos. Choose from side dishes of grated cheese, pineapple pieces, soured cream, chopped spring onions, lettuce torn up into shreds and chopped-up tomatoes.

Ingredients for 6 to 8 tacos

- 450 g (1 lb) lean beef or Quorn mince
- 2 tablespoons tomato ketchup, or 1 200 g (7 oz) tin of chopped tomatoes
- 1 teaspoon brown sugar
- 200 ml (1/3 pint) water
- Pinch of salt
- 1/2 teaspoon cayenne pepper
- 1/2 teaspoon ground cumin
- Pinch of paprika (1/2 teaspoon makes the mixture quite spicy)
- Box of taco shells

1 Put the mince in a deep saucepan and brown it. Do this by putting it on a low heat and stirring it round until it has changed colour.

2 Add the other ingredients and simmer gently for 20 minutes, stirring occasionally to stop the mixture sticking to the pan. If it looks too dry, add a little more water as it's cooking.

3 Grill the taco shells very gently until they are warm. Put them on plates and spoon the mixture into them (it doesn't matter if some of it falls out on to the plate).

Chicken tikka kebabs
MILD CREAMY CURRIED CHICKEN FROM INDIA

This is a lovely smooth dish with just a hint of curry flavour. You need to start making it about an hour before you cook it, because the chicken needs to marinate (soak) in the sauce for a while. Serve the kebabs on top of plain rice and pour the sauce over the top. You will need 6 kebab sticks or skewers. If you have wooden sticks, you must soak them in water for a little while before you use them.

● **Ingredients for 6 kebabs**
✿ 4 boneless chicken breasts (ask an adult to skin and cube them)
✿ 110 g (4 oz) natural yoghurt
✿ 1 teaspoon sugar
✿ 1 teaspoon curry powder

● **Ingredients for sauce**
✿ 1 teaspoon curry powder
✿ 110 g (4 oz) natural yoghurt
✿ 150 g (5 oz) crème fraîche
✿ 1 teaspoon sugar

1 Mix the kebab ingredients together in a bowl and leave for at least an hour.

2 Thread the chicken onto skewers (the pieces are slippery, so do this over the bowl). Place them on a grillpan.

3 Mix all the sauce ingredients together in a small saucepan.

4 Ask an adult to show you how to cook the plain rice. About 10 minutes before it's ready, grill the chicken kebabs until they are well cooked (they will have some little burnt spots, which is fine).

5 Gently heat up the sauce, stirring all the time. Then put the rice and kebabs on plates (pick up the kebab ends with oven gloves) and pour on the sauce.

PINWHEEL SANDWICHES

Make these with sliced bread and soft spreads such as cream cheese or peanut butter.

1 Cut the crusts from the bread slices. Each slice will make 3 or 4 pinwheels, depending on how thick you cut them.

2 Put the spread on, with a little bit extra down the long edges to help the pinwheel stick. Roll the bread up into a long sausage shape. Wrap the rolls in foil and chill for about 30 minutes before slicing up into round penny shapes.

If you like, thread a couple of small pinwheels sideways onto a cocktail stick.

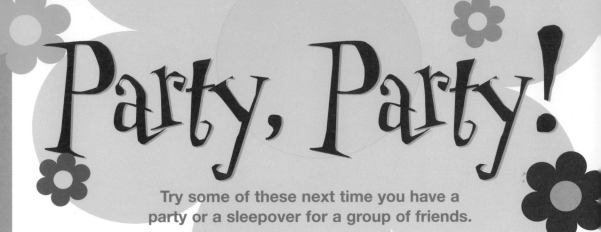

Party, Party!

Try some of these next time you have a party or a sleepover for a group of friends.

PARTY HEDGEHOG

This hedgehog makes a great party table display.

Ingredients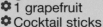
- 1 grapefruit
- Cocktail sticks
- Selection of pineapple chunks, cubes of cheese, mini tomatoes, chunks of grilled sausage
- 2 olives for eyes

1 Ask an adult to slice the bottom off the grapefruit so it will sit on a plate. Load the cocktail sticks with pieces of food and stick them all over the grapefruit.

2 Press in olives on sticks for eyes.

Spicy Nuts

Serve these cold in a bowl. They'll disappear really quickly! Leave out the Tabasco if you want a milder version.

Ingredients
- 1 tablespoon cooking oil
- 1 tablespoon soy sauce
- 1 beaten egg white
- Dash of Tabasco sauce
- 110 g (4 oz) shelled almonds or mixed shelled nuts

1 Put the oven on to 140°C (275°F, Mark 1).

2 Mix everything together in a bowl and spread the nuts on a baking sheet. Cook for 6 minutes, then ask an adult to get the tray out and stir the nuts round. Cook them for another 6 minutes.

26

HONEY POPCORN

Remember when you're popping popcorn... DON'T take the lid off the saucepan! If you do, you'll have a lot of clearing up to do.

Ingredients to make 1 bowl
❁ 50 g (2 oz) butter
❁ 2 tablespoons popcorn kernels
❁ 3 tablespoons clear honey

1 Put three-quarters of the butter into a large saucepan that has a lid. Melt the butter over a low heat. Then sprinkle the popcorn in and put the lid on.

2 Cook on a moderate heat, shaking the pan every now and again until there are definitely no more popping noises.

3 Put the rest of the butter in a frying pan and melt it gently with the honey. Stir the mixture into the popcorn. Turn the popcorn out onto a greased baking sheet and leave it to cool down.

HAVE A GREAT PARTY!
EXTRA IDEAS

◆ Buy some uncooked pizza bases. Cut shapes out of them with pastry cutters. Sprinkle the shapes with pasta tomato sauce and grated cheese and cook as per the base packet instructions.

◆ Buy mini pitta breads and put out bowls of ingredients such as grated cheese, tomato pieces, pineapple chunks etc. Let your guests build their own pitta sandwiches.

◆ Cut seedless grapes in half and sandwich them back together with cream cheese. If you like walnuts, you can sandwich them with cream cheese, too.

◆ Serve ideas from the snack section on pages 6-7, the mad food section on pages 44-45 and the sweet section on pages 28-29.

◆ Instead of serving party food on plates, grill lots of sausages and stick them all in one gigantic pile of mashed potato. Give each guest a spoon, a plate and a bowl of tomato sauce. Then ask them to dig in!

◆ Make some frosted drink glasses for your guests. Dip glass rims in beaten egg white and then in a bowl of caster sugar. The sugar will stick to the rim. If you like, mix food colouring into the sugar.

◆ Ask each guest to bring a plate of food. Then share everything out.

◆ Look out for fun sparklers that are designed to be stuck into food.

Party Ropes

Buy some coloured string or thin ribbon and tie on pretty wrapped sweets every few centimetres. You could tie on flat balloons and little presents, too (choose tiny ones). Give a rope to each friend as they leave, instead of a party bag.

Sweet Thoughts

Homemade sweets make great presents – they are extra-special because you have done them yourself.

CHOCOLATE KEBABS

Ingredients
- 175 g (6 oz) milk chocolate cake covering bar
- Mini marshmallows
- Glacé cherries
- Cocktail sticks
- Orange or similar to stick the kebabs in when drying

1 Ask an adult to help you melt the chocolate. You do this by breaking the chocolate into pieces in a small heatproof bowl. Stand the bowl in a saucepan filled with 5 cm (2 in) of water. Heat the water gently, stirring the chocolate until it melts. Ask an adult to lift the bowl out when ready.

2 Stick 2 mini marshmallows or a glacé cherry on the end of a cocktail stick and twirl it round in the chocolate. Stand the sticks in an orange so they can dry upright. Put them in the fridge to set.

NO-COOK FUDGE

If you like peanut butter, you'll love this old American recipe. This amount makes one large tin, plenty to give to all your friends.*

Ingredients
- 450 g (1 lb) icing sugar
- 2 tablespoons cocoa
- 225 g (8 oz) butter
- 1 dessertspoon peanut butter
- 1 teaspoon vanilla essence
- A pinch of salt

1 Sift the icing sugar and the cocoa into a bowl. Add all the ingredients and mix thoroughly.

2 Pack the mixture into a large greased tin and leave it in the fridge to set. Cut it into small pieces.

*You could put a few pieces in small plastic sandwich bags for your friends. However, warn them that there are nuts in the recipe as some people cannot eat them.

More Chocolate Dreams

Dip semi-dried fruit into melted chocolate. You can buy bags of it in supermarkets. Pears are especially delicious with chocolate sauce.

Mix 75 g (3 oz) of chopped almonds, raisins or 50 g (2 oz) desiccated coconut into melted chocolate. Then spoon the mixture into mini sweet cases and let it set in the fridge.

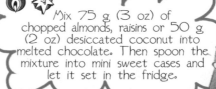

SWEETIE BASKETS

Wrap a few sweets in tissue paper and put them in pretty paper baskets as lovely gifts.

WHAT YOU NEED
✿ Medium-thickness paper in different colours
✿ Tracing paper, scissors, pencil and ruler
✿ Glue and glue brush

① Trace over the basket shape shown below. Turn over your tracing paper and scribble over the lines to transfer them to the coloured paper.

② Cut out the shape and fold it inwards along all the edges marked on our shape with dotted lines.

③ Glue the little tabs inside the basket and stick on a strip of paper 2.5 x 12 cm (1 x 5 in) to make a handle.

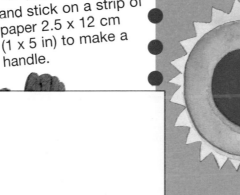

CREAMY CANDIES

You can flavour these little sweets with peppermint, or use flavoured icing sugar. Add different food colourings, too.

Why not make these yummy sweets as a surprise present for your best friend?

Ingredients for about 10 sweets
❉ 225 g (8 oz) icing sugar
❉ 3 tablespoons evaporated milk
❉ Green food colouring
❉ Peppermint essence

① Sieve the icing sugar into a bowl. Stir in the milk to make a smooth paste. Add the colouring and flavouring, too.

② Sprinkle some icing sugar on a board and knead the mixture for a little while. Use your knuckles to push down on the dough and fold it over several times.

③ Pull off pieces of the mixture and make into small shapes. Place them carcfully in mini sweet cases.

Decorating Ideas
● Glue coloured paper shapes on.

● Use a silver or gold decorating pen to write on the basket.

● Tie decorating ribbon round the top of the handle.

Minty ice bombe

Freeze this mixture for at least 3 hours to make a crunchy, ice cold pud.

Ingredients
🌼 2 packets of Dream Topping dessert mix
🌼 3 mini meringue nests (you can buy these in packets)
🌼 10 After Eight mints, cut into small pieces with scissors

1 Make up the Dream Topping as shown on the packet. Put it into a bowl.

2 Break the meringue nests into pieces and stir them in, together with the chocolate pieces.

3 Put the pudding in the freezer. Get it out 10 minutes before you want to eat it. Dip the bowl quickly in hot water and then turn it upside-down on a plate. Bang the top until the pudding comes out.

Perfect Puddings

All these puddings are guaranteed to taste delicious!

SAUCER PANCAKES

Eat these with sugar and jam.

Ingredients for 8 pancakes
🌼 50 g (2 oz) butter or margarine
🌼 50 g (2 oz) caster sugar
🌼 2 eggs
🌼 50 g (2 oz) plain flour
🌼 275 ml (½ pint) milk

1 Grease a Yorkshire pudding tin (a tin with wide, shallow pattie shapes). Put the oven on to 190°C (375°F, Mark 5).

2 Beat the sugar and butter together in a bowl or in a food processor. It will gradually go light and creamy.

3 Gradually beat in the eggs and then the flour. Stir in the milk (don't worry if it doesn't look smooth).

4 Spoon the mixture into the tin, filling each pattie shape about half full.

5 Bake for 15-20 minutes (the pancakes should be brown, but not burnt). Turn them out and sprinkle sugar over them. Put a spoonful of jam on each one.

PINK VELVET

Decorate this smooth raspberry mousse with spectacular chocolate leaves.

Ingredients

- 1 400 g (14 oz) tin of raspberries in juice
- 1 box of raspberry jelly
- 1 200 g (7 oz) tin evaporated milk
- 1 125 g (5 oz) pot of double or whipping cream for decoration

1 Put the raspberries and juice in a food processor to make them into a purée. Then press the purée through a sieve to get the pips out.

2 Make up the jelly to 275 ml

(½ pint) and leave it to cool. Then mix it with the raspberry purée and leave it in the fridge until it is just beginning to set.

3 Meanwhile whip the evaporated milk until it is thick. Fold it into the just-setting raspberry mixture and put it back in the fridge to finish setting.

4 To decorate the mousse, put teaspoonfuls of whipped cream around the edge and stick chocolate leaves into the cream.

MAKING CHOCOLATE LEAVES

Chocolate leaves always look really flash, but they're actually quite easy to make when you know how. To create them you need a few rose leaves and some plain cooking chocolate.

◆ First wash and dry the leaves, then ask an adult to help you melt the chocolate on the stove. (see page 28 to find out how).
◆ Lightly wipe the top side of each leaf over the melted chocolate.
◆ Lay the leaf on a plate and when the chocolate begins to harden gently peel the leaf away — you'll be left with perfect chocolate leaves!
◆ When you've made a batch, you can store them in a plastic box until you want them.

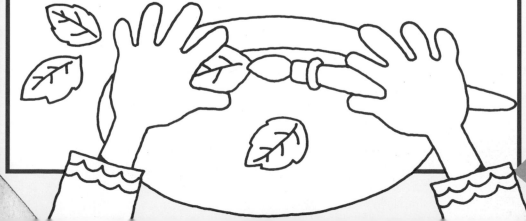

TOP TRIFLE

Trifle has been popular for many, many years. That's because it's fantastic! Trifle's fun to make because you build it up out of different ingredients.

Ingredients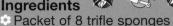

- Packet of 8 trifle sponges
- Jam
- 2 medium-sized tins of raspberries or strawberries in juice
- Box of ready-made custard (you need 425 ml, ¾ pint)
- Big carton (about 275 ml, ½ pint) double cream
- Hundreds and thousands to decorate the top

1 Ask an adult to cut the sponges in half. Spread them with jam and arrange them jam-side up in the bottom of a big pudding dish.

2 Pour the raspberries or strawberries and juice on top. Leave in the fridge for about 30 minutes so the juice soaks into the sponge.

3 Pour on the custard and then whip the cream and spoon it on. Just before you eat it, decorate the top with hundreds and thousands.

For a special party: Use angelica (green candied sticks), glacé cherries and flaked almonds to make a picture on the top of the trifle.

Food Traditions of the World

● Many people around the world are vegetarian. People of the Buddhist faith do not eat meat, for example.

● Visitors are offered special food and drink in many parts of the world. For example, Amazonian Indians might offer you a drink made from manioc root, water and human spit. The Turag people of the Sahara Desert would offer you sweet minty green tea. Everyone is expected to drink 3 cupfuls, and to refuse is thought very rude.

● People of the Islamic faith celebrate the festival of Ramadan, when they fast during the day and only eat at night.

● In Switzerland after Midnight Mass on Christmas Eve people drink hot chocolate and share huge homemade doughnuts called *ringli*.

● If you are collecting world food recipes (see pages 20-25) keep an eye out for food traditions, too. Write them in your notebook when you hear about them.

BE SANTA'S CHRISTMAS HELPER
There's a lot of food to prepare over Christmas, so it's a good time to ask if you can help out with these ideas.

Celebrate!

Food plays an important part in celebrations and festivals all over the world. Here are some recipes to add terrific taste to your special occasions.

CHOCOLATE LOG

Ingredients
✿ 75 g (3 oz) butter
✿ 175 g (6 oz) chocolate-flavoured icing sugar
✿ 1 to 2 tablespoons warm water
✿ 1 chocolate Swiss roll

1 Leave the butter on a plate to soften while you sift the icing sugar into a bowl through a sieve.

2 Beat the butter and the icing sugar together (in a bowl or a food processor). Add enough water to turn it into a thick paste.

3 Put the Swiss roll on a plate and spread the icing over it with a knife. Decorate the roll with icing shapes.

ICING SHAPES

Use these to decorate your log and make little presents.

Ingredients
✿ 1 packet ready-made white fondant icing
✿ Food colouring if you like

Pull pieces off the block of fondant to make all kinds of shapes. If you want to colour bits of it, knead food colouring in.

Sugar balls for buttons and eyes

Liquorice string for scarf

Flat shapes such as holly cut from rolled-out icing with food colouring added to it.

Shelled almonds for ears

Currants for eyes and nose

Liquorice tail

EASTER BISCUITS

These traditional biscuits have been made by generations of children. Join in the fun!

Ingredients for about 16 biscuits
* 110 g (4 oz) butter
* 110 g (4 oz) caster sugar
* 1 egg (separate it into white and yolk)
* 200 g (7 oz) plain flour
* Pinch of salt
* ½ teaspoon mixed spice
* ½ teaspoon cinnamon
* 4 tablespoons currants
* 1 to 2 tablespoons milk

1. Grease 2 baking sheets and put the oven on at 200°C (400°F, Mark 6).

2. Beat together the butter and sugar. When the mixture is pale and creamy, beat in the egg yolk.

3. Sift the flour, salt and spices into the mixture and stir in, then add the currants. Pour in enough milk to make a soft ball of dough.

4. Sprinkle flour on a board and knead the dough lightly. Then roll it out and use a cookie cutter to cut the dough into circles about 5 cm (2 in) wide.

5. Bake for 10 minutes. Then brush the biscuits with egg white and sprinkle extra caster sugar on top. Put them back in the oven for 10 more minutes until they are golden brown.

SAUSAGE AND BACON ROLLS

Make these to have with Christmas lunch. Prepare them the day before, and leave them in the fridge. Ask the main cook to put them in the oven on the day. That way you can stay out of the busy kitchen and enjoy yourself!

Ingredients
* Rindless streaky bacon (each slice will make 2 rolls)
* Pack of small sausages

1. Ask an adult to cut the bacon slices in half lengthways.

2. Put the slices on a board and run a knife over them to flatten them out and stretch them.

3. Roll a bacon piece around each sausage and lay the rolls on a baking tray with the end of the bacon tucked underneath.

4. Bake for 40 minutes at about 180°C (350°F, Mark 4). The oven will probably be on for the turkey anyway.

APPLE AND HONEY COMPÔTE FOR ROSH HASHANA

Rosh Hashana is the Jewish New Year celebration, held some time during autumn (the date changes). This traditional recipe is eaten during the two-day festival. It symbolises a good, sweet year.

Ingredients for 6 helpings
* 900 g (2 lb) baking apples
* 2 tablespoons lemon juice
* 220 ml (8 fl oz) honey
* ¼ teaspoon nutmeg
* 55 ml (2 fl oz) orange juice

1. Put the oven on at 190°C (375°F, Mark 5).

2. Ask an adult to peel and core the apples and cut them into quarters. Put them in a baking dish.

3. Mix together the other ingredients and pour them on the apples. Bake uncovered for 45 minutes.

Scrumptious Cakes

On these pages you'll find a mouth-watering assortment for cake lovers everywhere.

WORLD'S BEST FLAPJACKS

This recipe is utterly delicious (and very sticky).

Ingredients for 1 swiss roll tray
* 110 g (4 oz) butter
* 75 g (3 oz) golden syrup
* 75 g (3 oz) soft brown sugar
* 225 g (8 oz) rolled oats

1 Grease a 20 x 30 cm (8 x 12 in) Swiss roll tray. Put the oven on to 180°C (350°F, Mark 4).

2 Put the butter, syrup and sugar into a saucepan and heat them very gently until they have melted. Take them off the heat and mix in the oats.

3 Spread the mixture out on the tray and bake for 30 minutes, until golden brown.

4 After 5 minutes, while the mixture is still warm and soft, cut it into fingers. Then leave it to cool before you take it out of the tin.

LEMON CAKE

Bake this sponge cake in a loaf tin. Then put on the topping – the cake will soak it up.

For sponge:
* 175 g (6 oz) soft margarine
* 175 g (6 oz) self-raising flour
* 1 teaspoon baking powder
* 175 g (6 oz) caster sugar
* 2 eggs
* 3 tablespoons milk

For topping:
* Grated rind and juice of a lemon (ask an adult to show you how to do this)
* 110 g (4 oz) caster sugar

1 Grease a loaf tin and put the oven on at 180°C (350°F, Mark 4).

2 Put all the cake ingredients into a food processor and mix them together.

3 Put the mixture in the tin and bake it for about 50 minutes, until it has risen and springs back when you push it gently down with your finger.

4 Mix up the topping and pour it over the hot cake. Then leave it to cool and slice it up.

Chocolate Biscuit Cake

Make a slab of this and break it up into yummy pieces.

Ingredients for 1 sandwich tin
- 175 g (6 oz) Rich Tea biscuits
- 50 g (2 oz) butter
- 2 tablespoons golden syrup
- 50 g (2 oz) icing sugar
- 25 g (1 oz) drinking chocolate

1 Put the biscuits in a clean, clear plastic bag (such as a sandwich bag) and bash them with a rolling pin to break them up.

2 Put the butter and syrup in a saucepan and melt them gently. Take the saucepan off the heat and mix in everything else.

3 Press the mixture into the tin and leave it to set in the fridge.

Sweet as Sugar

You can buy several different types of sugar. For instance, granulated sugar has big grains, caster sugar has fine grains and icing sugar is so fine it looks like flour. For cake baking it's best to use fine caster sugar.

Vanilla Sugar

Vanilla is a sweet flavour that works really well in cakes. It comes from the pods of a plant. Buy a vanilla pod and store it in a jar of caster sugar that you use to bake cakes. It will transfer its flavour to the sugar and then to the cakes you cook. Top up the jar with more sugar each time you use some.

MINI CAKES

Make these little cakes for decorating (see over the page). If you like sultanas, add 50 g (2 oz) to the mixture.

Ingredients for 12-16 cakes
- 110 g (4 oz) butter or margarine
- 110 g (4 oz) caster sugar
- 2 eggs (beaten with a fork)
- 110 g (4 oz) self-raising flour
- Cake cases

1 Spread the cake cases on a tin and put the oven on at 190°C (375°F, Mark 5).

2 Beat the butter and sugar together and when the mixture is creamy add the eggs a little at a time. Then add the flour.

3 Spoon the mixture into the cake cases to make them two-thirds full.

4 Bake the mini cakes for about 15 minutes, until they are golden coloured.

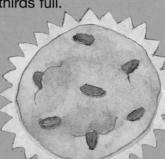

WHY WASH?

Always wash your hands before cooking, as dirty fingers can easily transfer germs onto the food you're preparing. Just remember this motto every time you go in the kitchen — "Wash well... ...Cook well!"

AMERICAN CREAM CHEESE FROSTING

This US icing is a tasty way of sandwiching cakes together. It can also be spread over the top.

Ingredients for spreading on 1 sponge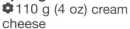
❀ 110 g (4 oz) cream cheese
❀ 50 g (2 oz) butter or margarine
❀ 175 g (6 oz) icing sugar
❀ 1 teaspoon vanilla essence

1 Leave the cheese and butter out on plates to soften them.

2 Beat all the ingredients together (a food processor is easiest). Now your icing is ready to use.

Nice Icing

Icing and cake decorating are lots of fun. You can make them as simple or as complicated as you like.

ARTISTIC ICING

You can paint on fondant icing using food colouring and clean paintbrushes. Buy a packet of ready-made white fondant icing. The paste-type food colouring is best because you can squeeze it onto a plate to use as a paint palette.

1 Bake a batch of mini cakes from page 35.

2 Roll out the icing on a board dusted with icing sugar. Cut out rounds to fit the top of your cakes (use a cake case as a cutter guide). When the mini cakes are cool, brush them with a little jam and stick an icing lid on each one.

3 Paint whatever you like on each cake. Then put them in the fridge to let the paint dry.

Very Easy Glacé Icing

Glacé icing is shiny and thin. For one batch, sift 110 g (4 oz) of icing sugar into a bowl and add just enough warm water to make a mixture that coats the back of your spoon like runny glue. Add teaspoonfuls of water until the mixture is right, and colouring, too, if you like. Use the icing straightaway.

Try dividing the icing into separate teacups and colour each batch differently. Then ice a batch of cakes and make them multicoloured.

You can flavour glacé icing by substituting fruit juice or cocoa dissolved in water for the plain water.

ALL ABOUT PIPING

If you like icing cakes, ask if you can try using a piping bag with a nozzle on the end. There are lots of different-shaped nozzles for making all kinds of shapes and lines of icing. Fill the bag half full with butter icing. If it's too full, it's hard to squeeze. Hold one hand under the bag and squeeze with the other to make the icing come out.

Practise a little bit of piping on some greaseproof paper before you actually do it on a cake.

Some piping effects

10 BRILLIANT CAKE DECORATING IDEAS

- Make flowers by sticking shelled almond halves into icing, round half a glacé cherry.

- Buy some icing pens. They make cake decorating really simple!

- Make some chocolate leaves from page 31. Stick them into chocolate butter icing.

- Make some fondant icing shapes to put on your cakes (see page 32).

- Run a fork over butter icing to make lines. You could wiggle them or swirl them round, too.

- Melt some cake-covering chocolate (see page 28). Spread it on a sponge cake. When it is set you could pipe vanilla-flavoured butter icing on top!

- Try white chocolate cake covering with chocolate butter icing piped on top.

- Press your favourite sweets onto icing.

- Sprinkle some desiccated coconut on top of icing.

- Put a teaspoonful of icing sugar in a sieve or a teastrainer and shake it over the top of your cakes.

BUTTER ICING FOR PIPING

Ingredients to ice one tray of mini cakes
- 225 g (8 oz) sifted icing sugar
- 110 g (4 oz) of butter, left out to soften

1. Beat the icing sugar and the butter together. If you like, add flavouring or food colouring. If you prefer, you can also use pre-flavoured icing sugar.

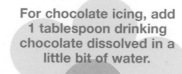

For chocolate icing, add 1 tablespoon drinking chocolate dissolved in a little bit of water.

For orange or lemon icing, add 1 teaspoon of fruit juice.

For vanilla icing, add a few drops of vanilla essence.

37

FOOD FAVOURITES

Write down your favourite food and ask your family what their favourites are, too. That way you'll be able to treat them by choosing recipes that you know they'll like.

Name
....

Favourite Food
....

Name
....

Favourite Food
....

Name
....

Favourite Food
....

Name
....

Favourite Food
....

Name
....

Favourite Food
....

Name
....

Favourite Food
....

Name
....

Favourite Food
....

Name
....

Favourite Food
....

Name
....

Favourite Food
....

Name
....

Favourite Food
....

The Best Biscuits

Biscuits are great for fast cooking fun. They don't take long to make and they get eaten quickly, too!

MONSTER FRISBEES

These cookies are so big they would satisfy any cookie monster!

Ingredients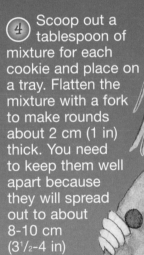
for 6-8 cookies (depending on how big you make them)
- 110 g (4 oz) soft butter or margarine
- 110 g (4 oz) light brown sugar
- 50 g (2 oz) white sugar
- 1 egg
- 110 g (4 oz) plain flour
- ½ teaspoon baking powder
- 2 packets (about 150 g/5 oz) of chocolate chips or buttons

(1) Put the oven on at 190°C (375°F, Mark 5). Grease a couple of big cooking trays (you may need 3 smaller ones).

(2) Beat the butter and sugars together until the mixture is smooth and creamy. Then mix in the egg.

(3) Sift the flour and baking powder into the bowl and mix them in. Then stir in the chocolate pieces.

(4) Scoop out a tablespoon of mixture for each cookie and place on a tray. Flatten the mixture with a fork to make rounds about 2 cm (1 in) thick. You need to keep them well apart because they will spread out to about 8-10 cm (3½-4 in) wide.

(5) Bake for 15 minutes, until the cookies are golden-coloured. Let them cool before you eat them.

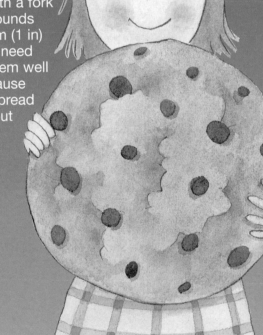

GINGERBREAD PEOPLE

Use a person-shaped cookie cutter to make these biscuits into people shapes, or cut shapes out yourself using the point of a knife. Once the biscuits have cooled, use icing pens to draw hair and clothes on them. Store uneaten biscuits in a plastic box.

Ingredients for 16 biscuits
- 350 g (12 oz) plain flour
- 1 teaspoon bicarbonate of soda
- 2 teaspoons ground ginger
- 110 g (4 oz) butter or margarine, cut into pieces
- 175 g (6 oz) soft brown sugar
- 1 beaten egg
- 4 tablespoons golden syrup
- Currants for eyes and buttons

1 Put the oven on at 190°C (375°F, Mark 5). Grease a couple of baking sheets.

2 Sift the flour, bicarbonate of soda and ginger into a mixing bowl. Use the tips of your fingers to rub in the butter until the mixture looks like breadcrumbs.

3 Stir in the sugar, then the egg and the golden syrup.

4 Dust a board with flour and knead the dough. Then roll it out to about 10 mm (½ in) thick.

5 Cut out the people and put them on the baking sheet. Push in currants for eyes and buttons. Bake for 12-15 minutes, until golden brown.

1-2-3 BISCUITS

Cut these little shortbread biscuits into finger shapes and use them to dip into ice cream or jelly.

Ingredients for 10 biscuits
- 25 g (1 oz) caster sugar
- 50 g (2 oz) butter
- 75 g (3 oz) plain flour

1 Put the oven on at 150°C (300°F, Mark 2). Grease 2 baking sheets. Then beat the sugar and butter together until the mixture is soft and creamy. Mix in the flour to make a ball of dough.

2 Sprinkle a board with flour and knead the dough a little (see page 14). Then leave it in the fridge for 10 minutes.

3 Roll the dough out and cut it into finger shapes. Bake them for 25 minutes, until they are light golden-coloured. When they are cool, sprinkle a little caster sugar on them.

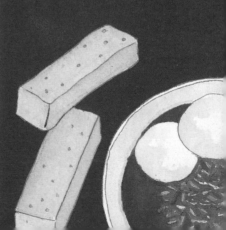

FLOWERS AND SMILES

On page 33 there is a recipe for Easter Biscuits. Make up a batch without the currants and spices. Then roll out the mixture and try these cookie-cutting ideas:

◆ Make Girl Talk flower-shaped biscuits. Use a flower-shaped cookie cutter or cut round your own flower shape with the point of a knife. When you have cooked and cooled the biscuits decorate them with icing pens.

◆ To make smiley faces cut out lots of round biscuits. Then use a knife to cut 2 eyes and a mouth out of half of the biscuits. When they are cooked and cooled, spread jam onto the plain biscuits and push the face biscuits down onto the jam.

ANYONE FOR A WORM?

Navy ships once carried a store of biscuits called 'hard tack', given out to the sailors as part of their rations. After some time at sea, the biscuits often got infested with worms. The sailors used to bang the biscuits on a table to make the worms drop out!

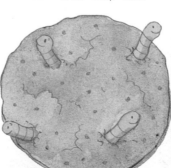

HOT CHOCOLATE SAUCE

This sauce is so gorgeous there are no words to adequately describe it...

Ingredients
- 25 g (1 oz) butter or margarine
- 25 g (1 oz) cocoa powder
- 1/2 teaspoon vanilla essence
- 2 tablespoons water
- 25 g (1 oz) sugar
- 1 tablespoon golden syrup

1 Put all the ingredients in a saucepan and heat gently, stirring with a wooden spoon until smooth. Don't boil the sauce or it will lose its shiny appearance.

2 Pour the warm sauce onto ice cream and eat it straight away.

Ice Cream Heaven

Make your own version of ice cream, create a fabulous sauce to pour on top or build your own unique ice cream sundae that looks as amazing as it tastes.

BANANA AND MARSHMALLOW ICE CREAM

Ingredients
- 110 g (4 oz) plain marshmallows
- 150 ml (1/4 pint) milk
- 4 ripe bananas
- 1 tablespoon lemon juice
- 275 ml (1/2 pint) whipped double cream or evaporated milk
- 1 or 2 teaspoons of sifted icing sugar (optional)

1 Put the marshmallows and milk in a saucepan and gently heat until the marshmallows melt. Let the mixture cool.

2 Mash the bananas with the lemon juice. Then mix them into the marshmallows along with the cream. Try the mixture and, if you want, add a little sifted icing sugar to make it sweeter.

3 Pour the mixture into a plastic box and freeze it overnight. Take out the box a quarter of an hour before you want to eat the ice cream, so it softens a little bit.

■ If you like, use chocolate marshmallows and add some grated chocolate.

BUTTERSCOTCH FUDGE SAUCE

This sauce can be kept in the fridge until you want it. Serve hot or cold.

Ingredients
- 75 g (3 oz) butter
- 225 g (8 oz) brown sugar
- 2 tablespoons golden syrup
- 1 small can evaporated milk

Melt the butter gently in a saucepan. Then add the sugar and syrup and stir over a gentle heat with a wooden spoon until smooth. Blend in the evaporated milk.

HOW TO MAKE A BANANA SPLIT

Here's a quick recipe for a yummy dessert that takes just minutes to prepare. Start by splitting a banana in half lengthways. Spoon ice cream into the middle. Add cream, sauce, grated chocolate, tinned fruit, nuts or whatever you fancy, then tuck in!

BUILD A SUNDAE

Find a tall sundae dish. Then spoon in ice cream with your favourite toppings and flavours sandwiched in between. Here are some sundae ideas:

- Hundreds and thousands
- Tinned fruit
- Chocolate drops
- Fruit puréed (pushed through a sieve) with a little icing sugar to sweeten it.
- Chocolate flakes
- Crushed chocolate cookies or ginger biscuits
- Whipped cream

Make sundae decorations and stick them in the top of the ice cream.

WHAT YOU'LL NEED
- Thick scrap paper
- Scissors
- Stiff plastic straws
- PVA glue
- Felt-tip pens

1

Cut shapes out of paper and wrap them round the top of the straws. Glue both sides together.

1

2

Decorate flags with felt-tip pens.

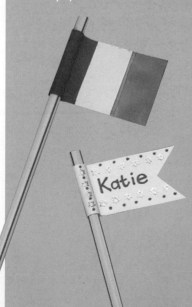

Katie

Come To Dinner

Use these recipes to cook a three-course dinner for your family or your friends. The starters and pudding are cold, so you can prepare them beforehand. One main course uses meat and one is a vegetarian dish.

STARTERS

Here are 3 ideas to choose from…

■ Make some **Dips** from pages 6-7.

■ **Bacon and Cheese Salad**: shred a crispy lettuce and put it in a big salad bowl with some small grilled bacon pieces and cubes of your favourite cheese. Toss the salad in the 'ensalade verde' dressing from page 21. Then ask your guests to help themselves to the bowl as a starter.

■ **Spicy Tuna**: mash 2 drained tins of tuna with 3 tablespoons of mayonnaise and a couple of chopped-up spring onions. If you like garlic, add a crushed clove. If you prefer a spicy taste, add some drops of Tabasco sauce. Put one or two small crispy lettuce leaves on every plate and pile tuna mixture into each one.

MAIN COURSES

CHICKEN AND BACON ROLLS

Serve warm with mashed potato mixed with grated cheese, boiled carrots tossed with a little butter and a teaspoon of brown sugar, and gravy made from granules.

Ingredients for 4 people
❁ 12 slices rindless streaky bacon
❁ 12 boneless, skinless chicken thighs (buy a pack in a supermarket)
❁ 110 g (4 oz) grated Cheddar cheese (ask an adult to help)
❁ Box of cocktail sticks

1 Put the oven on at 190°C (375°F, Mark 5).

2 Lay the bacon slices on a board and stretch them by running the back of a knife along them.

3 Lay the chicken thighs on top of the bacon pieces and flatten them out a little with a knife. Sprinkle the cheese on them.

4 Roll up the bacon and chicken and stick a cocktail stick through each one to make a roll. Put the rolls on a baking tray and bake for 35 minutes.

LEMON DELIGHT

DESSERT

Ingredients for 2 large desserts

- 1 225 g (8 oz) tub of cream cheese
- 1 200 g (7 oz) tin of sweetened condensed milk
- Grated rind and juice of a lemon (ask an adult to show you how to do this)
- 150 ml (¼ pint) whipped double cream

1 Mix all the ingredients apart from the double cream and sponges together in a food processor and spoon it into pretty bowls or glasses. Place the glasses in the fridge for 30 minutes to set.

2 Decorate each dessert with the cream and a sponge finger.

DECORATING THE TABLE

- Put a small vase of flowers on the dinner table.
- Make name cards for each setting by folding squares of card in half, decorating them and writing a guest's name on each one.
- Put a glass by each place setting. Roll up pretty paper napkins and stand one in each glass.

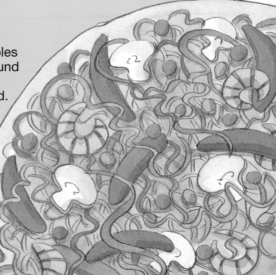

Oriental Stir-fry

Ingredients for 2 people

- 4 tablespoons light soy sauce
- 4 teaspoons runny honey
- 2 teaspoons of ginger
- 1 clove of garlic
- Packet of medium egg noodles (allow 1 layer of noodle per person)
- 2 tablespoons vegetable oil
- Packet of Quorn pieces
- Packet of fresh ready chopped stir-fry vegetables, available from all large supermarkets

1 Mix the soy sauce, honey, ginger and garlic in a cup.

2 Cook the noodles as instructed on the packet, while they are cooking, you can do the stir-fry.

3 To make a successful stir-fry, you should use a big wide pan called a *wok*. Ask an adult to heat up the oil for you in the wok and tip in the Quorn pieces. Use a wooden spoon to push the pieces around the pan for a couple of minutes.

4 Add the vegetables and stir them round for about 5 minutes, until they look cooked. Then add the soy sauce mixture and stir for a further minute.

5 Ask an adult to drain the noodles. Pile the noodles on plates, with some stir-fry on top.

Funny Food

Use these crazy cookery ideas for parties or times when your friends come round for tea.

MASHED POTATO DINOSAURS

Model a dinosaur body from cheesy mashed potato. Leave it until you're nearly ready to eat, then warm it up for 10 minutes in the oven. Add the sausages and beans just before you serve it.

Ingredients

✿ Packet of instant mash
(or a saucepan of mashed potato)
✿ Knob of butter
✿ 50 g (2 oz) grated cheese per model
(ask an adult to help)
✿ Box of cocktail sausages (you need 3 per model)
✿ Small can of baked beans

1. Grease an ovenproof dish. Make up the instant mash with the butter and the cheese (or stir the butter and cheese into fresh mashed potato if you prefer). If you like, add drops of green food colouring to the mash.

2. Use a teaspoon to spoon the potato onto the dish and model it with a knife. Start by spooning on a body, then a head. Add a tail and 4 legs. If you like, add a frilled collar round the neck and mark scales on the body using the end of your teaspoon.

3. When you're ready to eat, warm up your model for ten minutes in the oven at 180°C (350°F, Mark 4). While it warms, grill the sausages.

4. Take your model out and stick the sausages down its back. Press baked beans into the model for eyes and feet. Then spoon the rest of the beans around the outside and draw a tomato ketchup tongue.

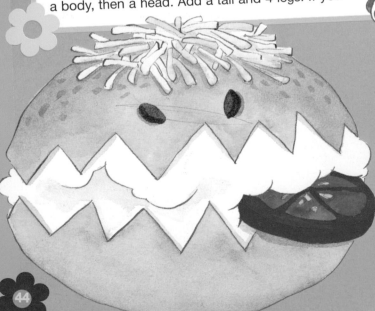

MONSTER ROLLS

Monster Rolls are great fun to make and really do look like scary creatures! Experiment with fillings to add different coloured and sized features to your monster.

1. Ask an adult to cut round a crusty roll using a sharp knife to make jagged teeth.

2. Put your favourite filling in the roll. Then use a piece of tomato to make a tongue and some grated cheese for hair. Push in raisins for eyes.

VOLCANO CAKE

Just before you serve this cake put 4 candle holders and birthday candles on the top. You could add food sparklers, too.

Ingredients
✿ Big bar of chocolate cake covering
✿ 350 g (12 oz) Choco Krispies
✿ Packet of Dream Topping
✿ Red food colouring
✿ Box of red-coloured jelly
✿ Red, yellow and black icing pens

1 Melt the chocolate cake covering (see page 28). Stir in the Choco Krispies.

2 Pile the mixture onto a plate to make a mountain shape (use a knife to help you model it). Make a hollow in the middle by pushing the end of a rolling pin down onto the mound. When you're happy with your shape, leave it in the fridge for 30 minutes to harden off.

3 Make up the Dream Topping and add drops of red food colouring to create 'lava'. Make up the jelly to 275 ml (½ a pint)

and chop it up when it has set.

4 Pile Dream Topping onto the volcano, dribbling it down the sides with a knife. Use your icing pens to draw volcano streams down the sides. Pile jelly on the top and around the base of the volcano.

MAD MENUS

Here are some tips to help you invent your own mad food ideas.

● Use food colouring to change the colour of cream, mashed potato or Dream Topping.

● Make eyes, mouths, ears and noses from vegetables and use cocktail sticks to anchor them in place. Remember to tell your guests to take out the sticks before they start eating.

● Sliced bread is easy to cut or roll into shapes.

● Sweets and raisins make good eyes.

● Buy boxes of pre-made fondant icing to make into funny edible shapes. Add any food colouring you like. You could make little green dinosaur babies to sit in Choco Krispie nest shapes (make the mixture as with the volcano cake).

● Set jelly in unusual shapes. Look out for fun jelly moulds.

Take a photo of any fun food you invent. Then stick it in your own recipe collection (see pages 46-47)

TOAST FACES

Cut a face out of cooking foil, with holes for the mouth and eyes. Lay foil on a slice of bread and toast the bread under the grill.

YUM YUM CRUNCH!

A Frenchman nicknamed Monsieur Mangetout has set many strange eating records since the 1960s by munching machinery, including bicycles, TV sets and a light aeroplane...

My Recipes

Use this space to write or stick in a few of
your own favourite recipes. Then this book will truly
be YOUR personal Girl Talk Book of Cooking.

Make your own recipe file

Start collecting recipes now. Ask for a recipe from each of your friends and family to get you started. Cut out ones you like from magazines.

1 Buy 4 plain-card A4-sized folders from a stationery shop.

2 Decorate them with felt-tip pens or by gluing on paper shapes. Give each one a different title:

'Starters and Main Courses'

'Cakes, Biscuits and Sweets'

'Puddings'

'Food from Around the World'

3 Store your recipes in the right folders, so they'll be easier to find. Tie your folders together with a long piece of coloured ribbon.

Index

Use this index to quickly search for the recipes you need. The entries in *italics* show food tips, ideas and make-its for you to try.